BATH
The Golden Years

From the archives of
THE BATH CHRONICLE

Theresa Ford and Karen Birch

HALSGROVE

The Bath Chronicle

First published in Great Britain in 2003

Images © 2003 *The Bath Chronicle*
(unless otherwise acknowledged)
Selection and text © 2003 Theresa Ford and Karen Birch

All rights reserved. No part of this publication may be reproduced, stored in a retrieval system, or transmitted in any form or by any means without the prior permission of the copyright holder.

British Library Cataloguing-in-Publication Data
A CIP record for this title is available from the British Library

ISBN 1 84114 304 9

HALSGROVE

Halsgrove House
Lower Moor Way
Tiverton, Devon EX16 6SS
Tel: 01884 243242
Fax: 01884 243325
email: sales@halsgrove.com
website: www.halsgrove.com

Printed and bound in Great Britain
by CPI Bath Press, Bath

CONTENTS

1	The Post-war City	7
2	Royal Visitors	25
3	City of Festivals	39
4	At Work	55
5	At Play	71
6	Changing Landscapes	87
7	Familiar Faces	115
8	The Weather	135
9	Sport	149

ACKNOWLEDGEMENTS

The majority of photographs in this book come from the archive at *The Bath Chronicle*. We are indebted to the team of *Chronicle* photographers who have worked hard over the years to capture these visual memories.

We would also like to thank everyone who helped us to identify people, places and events in the un-captioned file pictures, especially Christopher Hansford and Judy Boyd.

A special thanks goes to Peter Hall who helped us with the sports pictures and Terry Sowden and Stephanie Round at Bath Central Library who supplied several pictures.

❧ INTRODUCTION ❦

Our aim with this book is to trigger memories. We hope that these photographs of our city, of the people who have lived and visited and the places and landmarks which made Bath unique, will evoke memories of times gone by.

Some people may find themselves preserved within the pages, and others will recognise familiar faces or places.

For many readers the photographs will bring back memories of what they were doing on specific dates, Coronation Day, or the night the Beatles played at the Pavilion.

For those readers unfamiliar with our city, we hope the photographs give an insight into the events and people which have helped shape Bath into today's thriving historic city.

Inevitably, some of the buildings, traditions and people have been lost over the years, but these photographs will stand as a permanent record of a past way of life which will prove of interest to both present and future inhabitants and visitors.

David Gledhill
Editor, *The Bath Chronicle*

BATH – *The Golden Years*

Chapter One
THE POST-WAR CITY

In retaliation for the RAF raids on the historic German cities of Lubeck and Cologne, which took place in March 1942, the Germans blitzed equally historic British cities.

Bath, York, Canterbury, Norwich, and Exeter were all attacked during what came to be called the Baedeker raids, named after a famous tourist guidebook.

Bombing during the night of 25 April and the early hours of 27 April devastated the unprotected city, killing more than 400 men, women and children and destroying or damaging thousands of historic buildings.

The city's image as a place of safety changed but, despite the hardship and suffering, the event brought people together with a shared sense of common purpose.

There were parties across the city on Victory in Europe (VE) Day, 8 May 1945 and a triumphant editorial in *The Chronicle* declared 'Today, VE-Day, the world is enjoying itself for the war against Germany has been won.'

Inevitably, the end of the war was followed by many years of shortages. Food rationing continued until 1954, but slowly, over the years, conditions improved for the majority of people and the city moved forward towards a prosperous future.

Bath men registering as fire watchers.

Bomb-damaged shops in the Bear Flat area of Bath. April 1942.

A mobile canteen where the people of Bath who had lost their homes could get a hot drink.

All that remained of West Twerton School after the night of bombing. April 1942.

Fire takes hold of houses in Upper Bristol Road.

Homeless people carry their belongings from their bomb-ravaged homes to temporary accommodation.

THE POST-WAR CITY

Left in ruins. The rugby stand at the Recreation Ground.

A ray of hope over Bath Abbey. Viewed from where houses once stood on Wells Road.

Picture by Major Noel C Harbutt

Soldiers stand on guard to protect onlookers from the gaping hole left in Great Stanhope Street.

The Francis Hotel on the south side of Queen Square received a direct hit during the raids of April 1942.

THE POST-WAR CITY

Bombing destroyed this house on The Paragon.

Repairing the damage done to the younger Wood's masterwork, the Royal Crescent. Two houses on the Crescent were burnt out, but although a bomb made a huge crater in the roadway, the magnificent facade of the crescent was unimpaired.

THE POST-WAR CITY

Bombing destroyed this house on The Paragon.

Repairing the damage done to the younger Wood's masterwork, the Royal Crescent. Two houses on the Crescent were burnt out, but although a bomb made a huge crater in the roadway, the magnificent facade of the crescent was unimpaired.

THE POST-WAR CITY

Never to be replaced. The stunning St James's Church, which stood on the junction of Stall Street and Southgate Street, was built in Italian style. The copper dome of the 'pepper-pot' cupola, which blazed white hot, had to be pulled down.

The morning after. Householders in King Edward Road, Oldfield Park, survey the damage. Theirs was one of the worst hit districts in the city.

Wartime poster in The Circus, intended to help members of the public to identify the enemy.

THE POST-WAR CITY

A city treasure, the ancient Abbey Church House, which was all but demolished by a direct hit.

Many victims, both known and unknown, were mourned by the people of Bath at the Haycombe Cemetery.

Soldiers in Kingsmead Square after two nights of bombing.

THE POST-WAR CITY

Pack up your belongings. Householders and the Home Guard move possessions from bombed houses.

BATH – *The Golden Years*

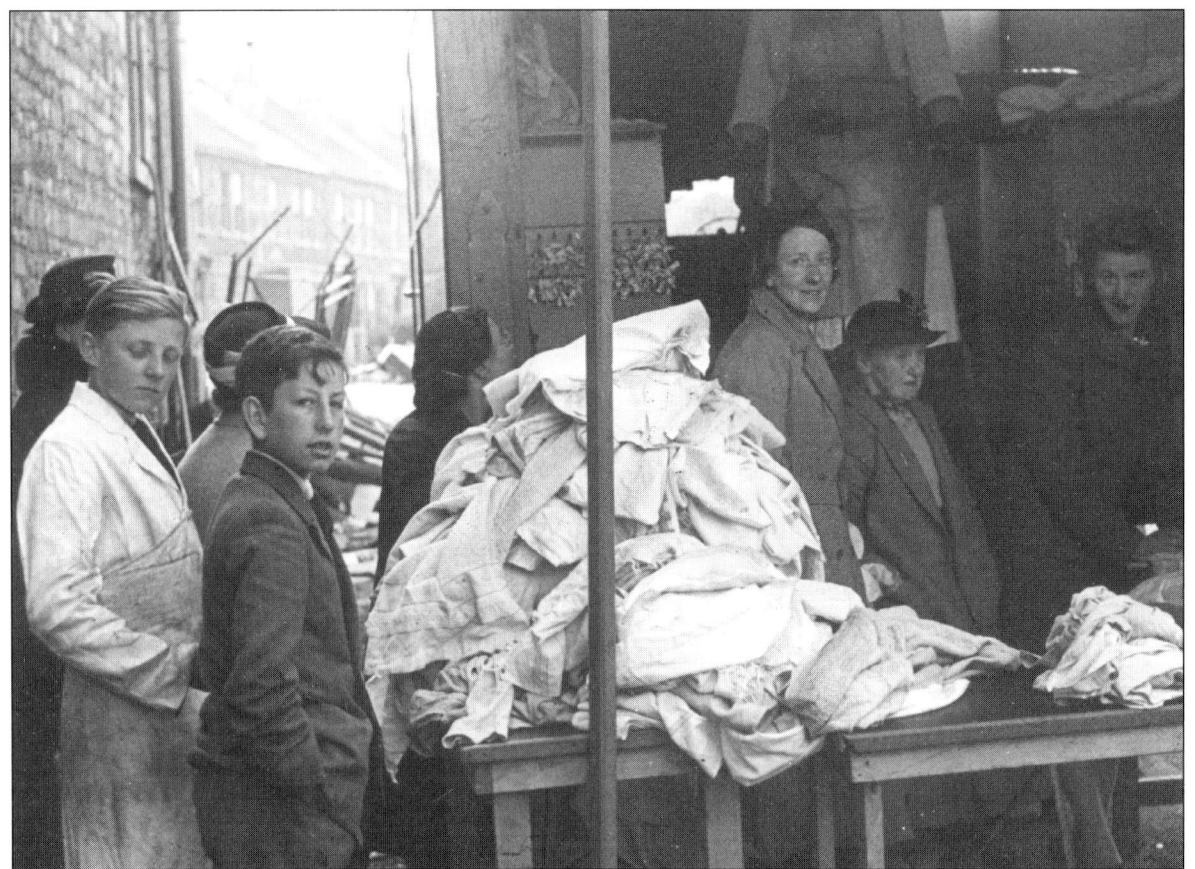

National emergency washing service depot at Oldfield Park where local residents could have their washing done.

St Bartholomew's in Oldfield Park, built in 1937, was the city's newest church when it was struck during the two nights of bombing.

THE POST-WAR CITY

VE-Day celebrations. A funfair on the Recreation Ground. May 1945.

Bathonians read the good news in their Bath & Wilts Chronicle and Herald. *Victory in Europe. May 1945.*

VE-Day street party. Dartmouth Avenue, Twerton.

THE POST-WAR CITY

Makeshift washing line rigged up by staff at the Pump Room restaurant.

All that's left from the houses on the Upper Bristol Road.

May 1942. After the mayhem of the bombing the previous month, water was still in short supply in homes. These two young girls happily go to fill their buckets.

Chapter Two
ROYAL VISITORS

Royal visits are always causes for celebration and the city has unfurled the banners and raised the royal flag on many occasions, both formal and informal.

In April 1942, after the city had endured two nights of bombing, King George VI and Queen Elizabeth visited the city and met the people during their visit.

BATH – *The Golden Years*

Princess Margaret taking the waters, at the Pump Room during her visit as patron of the first Bath International Music Festival. 1 May 1948.

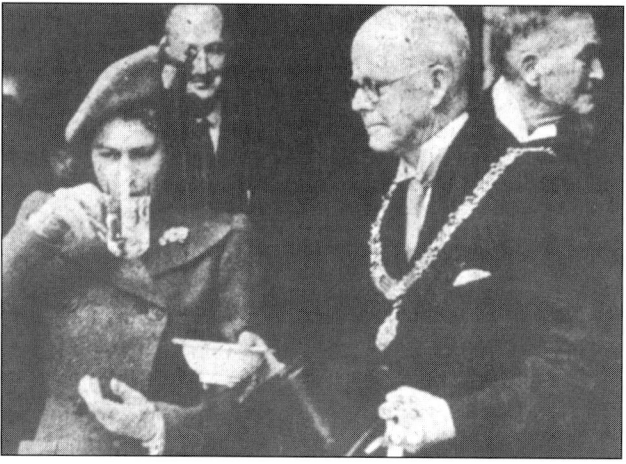

Princess Elizabeth takes the waters at the Pump Room. 1945.

ROYAL VISITORS

Princess Margaret, May 1948. The Chronicle described her appearance and clothes in great detail and noted that the predominant comment was 'How sweet and natural she is.'

Queen Elizabeth with the Mayor in the Guildhall, 1956.

The Queen Mother is greeted by a guard of honour of students at the newly opened College of Domestic Science in March 1960.

Princess Margaret at the Guildhall, 1962

At Bath Spa Railway Station, Princess Margaret and Lord Snowdon. February 1963.

Princess Margaret and Lord Snowdon after early morning communion at Widcombe Parish Church. They had been staying at Widcombe Manor, home of Mr and Mrs Jeremy Fry. With them are the vicar, the Rev. J.C. Armes (centre) and Rev. L.A. Hibbard. July 1963.

ROYAL VISITORS

Top and above: *Princess Anne at the Bath and West Show. May 1969.*

The Queen Mother. April 1970.

ROYAL VISITORS

Prince Charles meets the Brownies of Newton St Loe. June 1970.

Prince Phillip talking to the crowd during a visit. August 1973.

The Queen Mother presents the Babycham Gold Cup to Marion Mould at the Bath and West Show. Looking on are the Show president, Lord Digby and Mr Francis Showering. June 1976.

Happy smiles from the Queen Mother as she talks to W.Q. Roberts, show director during a visit to the Bath and West Show.

The Queen in the Parade Gardens during the fancy dress parade to mark her Silver Jubilee year. August 1977.

Alison Hayward and her friend Trisha Carpenter handed Prince Charles a flower and then cheekily claimed a kiss. 1980.

ROYAL VISITORS

Princess Margaret at the Theatre Royal. March 1988.

The Prince and Princess of Wales with their sons at a wedding at Bath Abbey. They were guests of the then BBC chairman Marmaduke Hussey, who lives at Chewton Mendip, for the wedding of his daughter, Katherine, to Sir Francis Brooke. April 1989.

Chapter Three
⋄ CITY OF FESTIVALS ⋄

The Bath International Music Festival has been attracting audiences since it was founded more than fifty years ago. The annual celebration of great music has included classical, early jazz, contemporary, world music and blues, and brought many acclaimed artists to the city.

In 1993 Bath Festivals Trust was created to build on the city's reputation as a festivals city and Bath now hosts a wide range of events.

The music festival has been joined by a week-long annual literature festival, a puppet festival, a film festival, a guitar festival and, of course, a Jane Austen festival.

Saturday, 1 May 1948. Princess Margaret was the first Patroness of the Bath Assembly, as the Bath International Music Festival was then known. The seventeen-year-old princess visited Bath for the festival's final day – a day which The Chronicle *renamed M-Day – M for Margaret and M for May Day.*

BATH – *The Golden Years*

June 1962. Putting the finishing touches to The Bucentaur, the Doge's barge, for the highlight of the 1962 festival, 'La Serenissima', an eighteenth-century Venetian evening held in Parade Gardens. Left to right are Sarah Hailstone, Mrs Charles Robertson, chairman of the committee organising the event, Mrs Hugh Crallan, Enid Hanks and Mrs Greville Cavendish.

Venetian singers, Umberto Da Prda and Stella Nory singing on the gondola.

CITY OF FESTIVALS

Guests masquerading as citizens of eighteenth-century Venice wore black masks, tricorn hats and gaily coloured cloaks. The guests' supper baskets contained strawberries and cream, smoked salmon and asparagus rolls. The rose wine was specially imported from the shore of Lake Garda, near Venice.

BATH – *The Golden Years*

Princess Margaret with Lord Snowdon and Ted Leather, chairman of the Festival Society, greeted at the Parade Gardens by Mrs V. Crallan, a member of the organising committee. June 1962.

Crowds waited patiently for three-and-a-half hours before Princess Margaret, Lord Snowdon and the official party arrived at the main entrance of Parade Gardens.

Yehudi Menuhin, Margot Fonteyn and Rudolf Nureyev on the stage of the Theatre Royal, after a specially choreographed performance of Bartok's Divertimento. *June 1964.*

The Arabian Banquet at the Bath Festival Fringe. July 1966.

Bath festival Fringe. Mr & Mrs Joseph Woods, Cllr & Mrs H. Caralland, and Mr & Mrs Peter Watts at the Two Sovereigns Ball. June 1969.

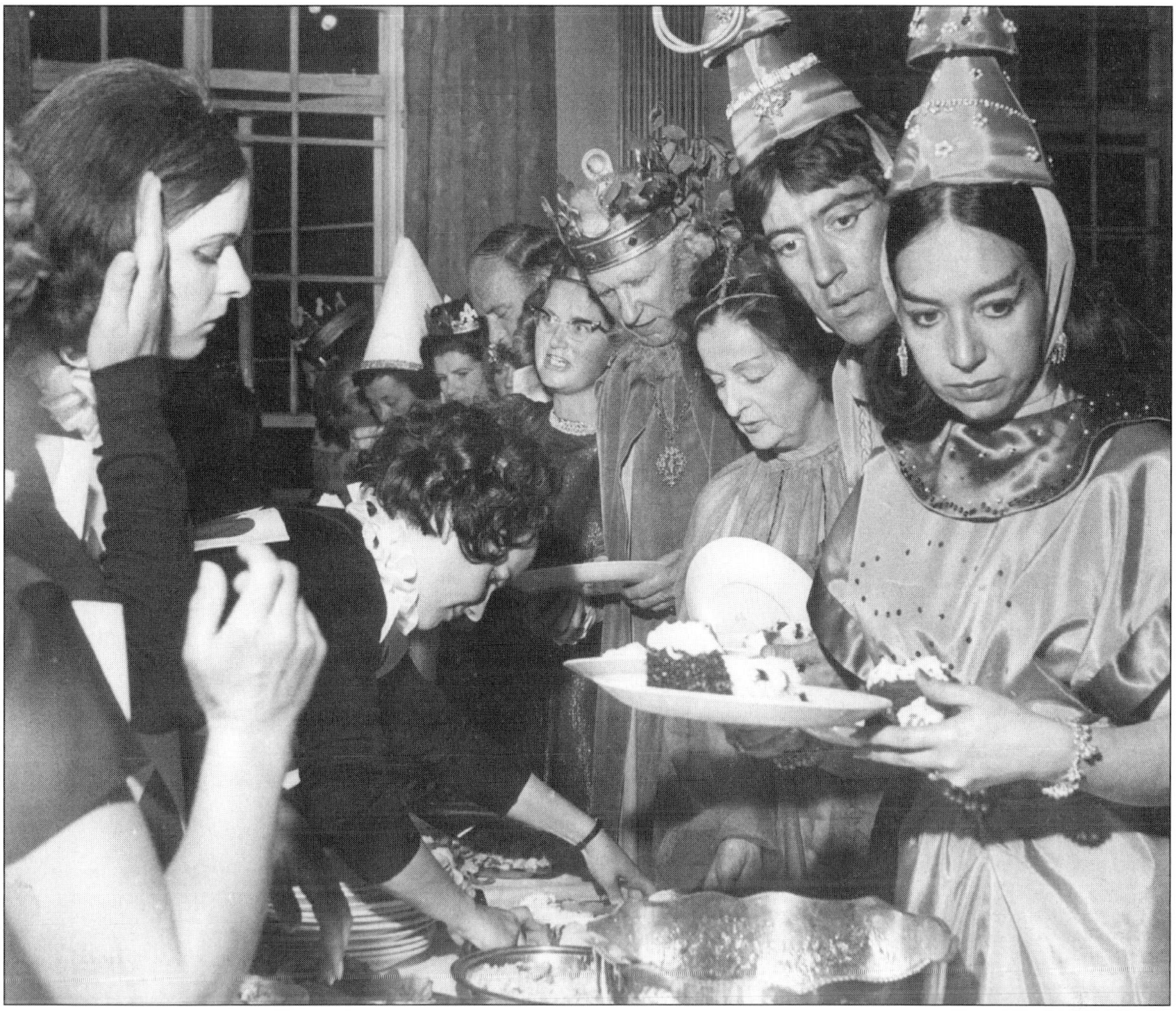

Diners queue for the banquet at The Two Sovereigns Ball.

Logo for the Bath Festival 1966.

A dais containing a festival flame built for the 1965 festival. A relay of athletes carried a burning torch through the city, trumpeters in colourful blue outfits sounded a fanfare and the drums rolled as the final runner came through the crowd to light the flame. Arnold Goodman, chairman of the Arts Council gave the inaugural address, describing the festival as an event of international repute. The flame burned in the Abbey Church Yard for the duration of the festival.

Signs welcoming visitors to the Bath Festival in 1969.

CITY OF FESTIVALS

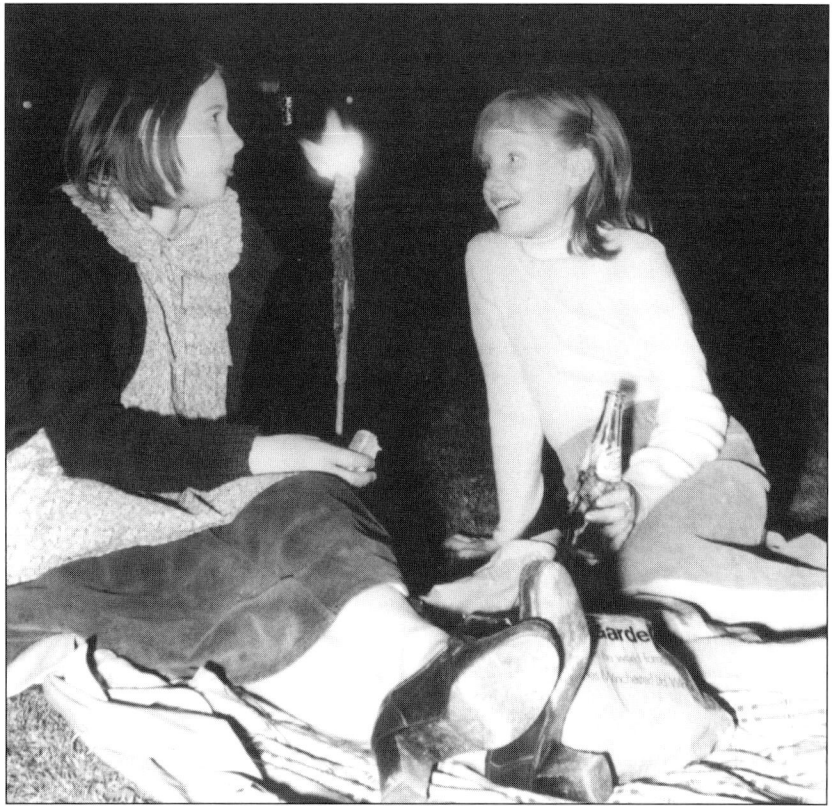

1978. Candles lined the streets from the Circus to the end of Royal Crescent for the festival. Sophie Jackman and Nicola Leighton-Thomas picnicked by candlelight on the Royal Crescent lawn.

Above: 1995. Julie Tanner, a pupil at Bathwick St Mary's School won third prize in the schools' writing competition, organised by the Bath Literature Festival.

Right: 1995. Rebecca Howell met Walker Bear from the Walker Books series during the first Literature Festival.

Above and opposite: *1969 Blues Festival.*

The first was held at the Recreation Ground in the centre of Bath. 7000 tickets were printed but more than 30,000 music fans descended on the city for the two days and nights of the event. Led Zeppelin, 10 Years After and Fleetwood Mac performed. After the event, letters flooded into The Chronicle *as locals complained about people sleeping rough on the streets and in shop doorways, milk bottle thefts from doorsteps and long-haired men.*

Above and opposite: *1970 Blues Festival.*

The city banned the use of the Recreation Ground for the Blues Festival after the furore and the following year it moved to the new permanent site of the Bath & West Show at Shepton Mallet. Fairport Convention, Pink Floyd and Steppenwolf, Santana, Frank Zappa, Canned Heat, Jefferson Airplane and The Byrds played in front of a crowd of 200,000. Among the audience was a young farmer, Michael Eavis who, the following year, organised his own music festival at his farm in Pilton near Glastonbury.

CITY OF FESTIVALS

Jazz made its first appearance on the Bath Festival programme in 1958 when a five-day Bath Festival of Jazz took place in the Regency Ballroom. Johnny Dankworth, a seasoned festival artist, appeared at the Jazz Festival many times over the years, both alone, and with his wife Cleo Laine, to the delight of local jazz aficionados.

Chris Barber.

CITY OF FESTIVALS

Acker Bilk, with Ted Leather, chairman of the Bath Festival Society, on the drums. June 1962. Almost 1400 jazz fans crammed into Bath's Regency Ballroom to see Somerset-born, black-bowlered, Acker Bilk. Hundreds more heard the concert broadcast on the BBC's Jazz Club programme, introduced by Derek Jones from the ballroom. The audience were the first to hear 'Coffee and Acker Cake', the theme from the recently completed film, 'Band of Thieves'.

Jazz at The Regency Ballroom mid '60s. In 1969 there was an all-night Carnival of Jazz at the Regency Ballroom. Guests paid 15 shillings to be entertained from 10.30pm to 7am. Ken Colyer, Alex Welsh, Mick Mulligan were all on the programme.

BATH – *The Golden Years*

An open-air performance at the Jazz Festival.

Chapter Four
⁓ AT WORK ⁓

Although Bath was never a great industrial city, the plentiful supply of water, local stone, local coal deposits and the proximity of the docks of Bristol, combined with three mainline rail links, ensured that several industries developed in the area.

Many have disappeared and often the buildings have been converted for a different use, but the names of plasticine maker, Harbutts, Bath Cabinet Makers, Carr's Mill and Stothert & Pitt are still familiar to most Bathonians. Bath has also had a long association with the Ministry of Defence since its staff relocated to the city in anticipation of the war.

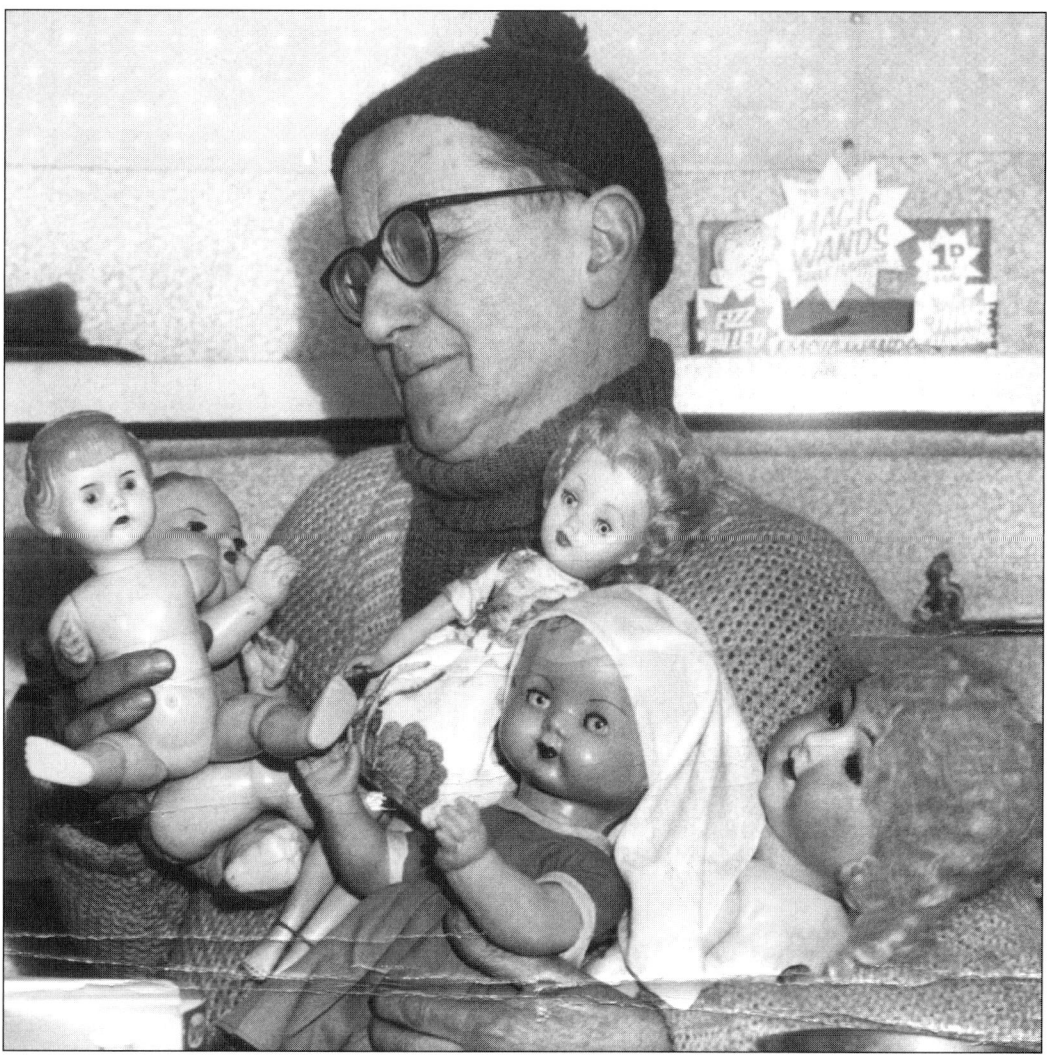

Leslie Law, known as Dr Kildare of Holloway, who ran the Holloway Dolls' Hospital. He took up doll repairs after a long stage career.

BATH – *The Golden Years*

Leonard Thickitt, the last sweetmaker at the Trowbridge firm, R.A. Wilkins. He had worked there for almost fifty years. The company was best known for its Winter Mixture and Mint Shrimps.

Mary and Livia Kiss, struggling to choose from the range of sweets at Deveralls George, Deveralls' cash and carry warehouse in Walcot Street. The firm introduced bubble gum to Bath in the 1930s.

AT WORK

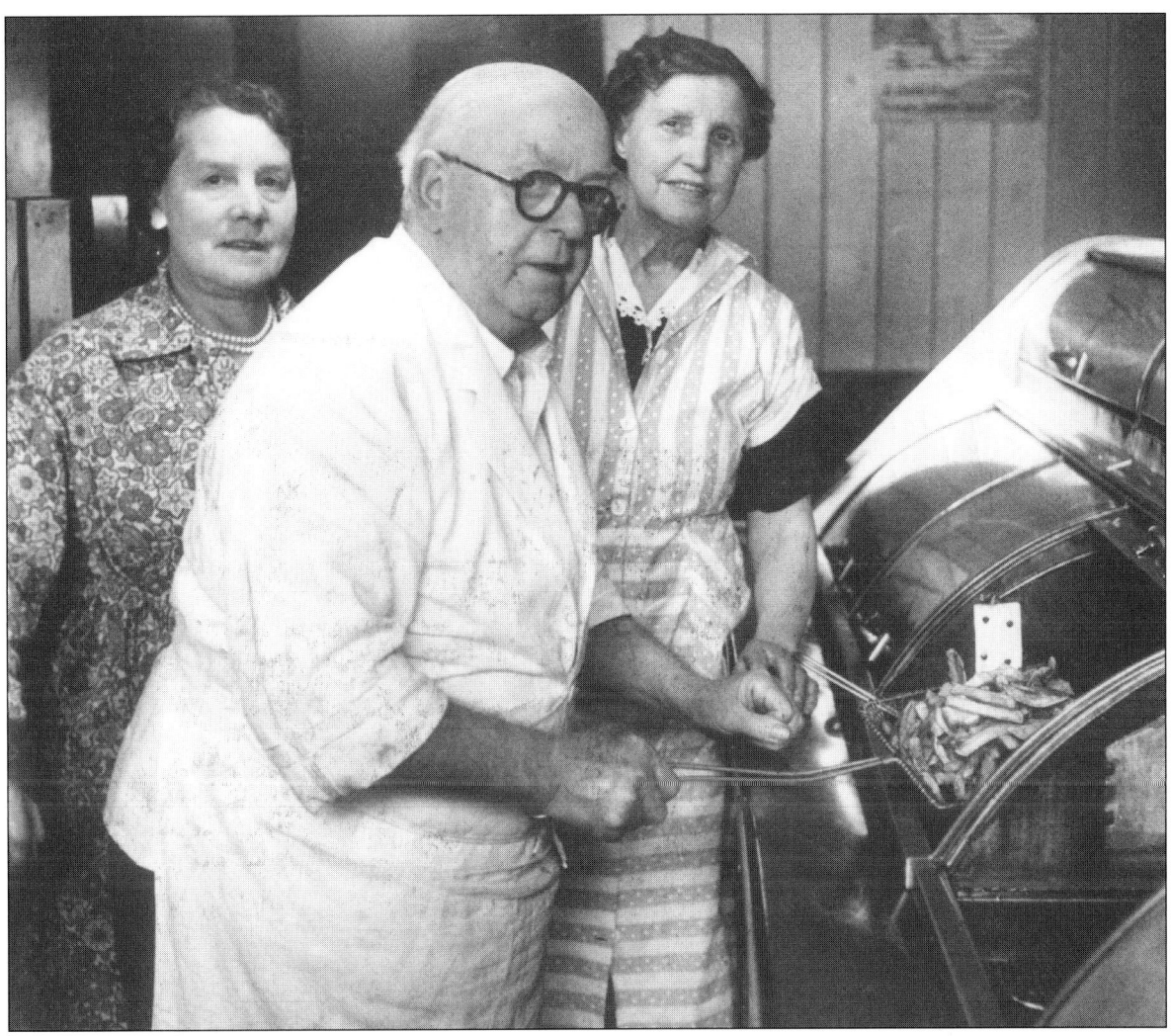

In June 1962, after thirty-five years in the trade, Mr Frank Meredith closed his fish and chip saloon in Holloway. He took over the saloon, which was in the lower end of Holloway between St Mark's Church parish room and the Dolls' Hospital in 1928. When he first started the business he bought old potatoes for 2s.9d a cwt.

Railway driver Arthur Cannings and fireman John Watts prepared the last steam shunter at Bath West Goods Station in May 1961.

Driver Arthur Cannings takes the last shunter out with his three passengers.

AT WORK

Postman Keith Costello collecting from the Emett-like post box in Great Pulteney Street in April 1970. The box was in danger of disappearing when the lock became worn out, until Chubb said they could make a copy if they could borrow the lock.

J.B. Bowler & Sons Ltd. on the corner of Corn Street was well-known as an invaluable source of supply for the kind of fittings and spare parts that nobody else seemed to have. Nothing was ever thrown away in the store, in the confidence that there was bound to be a customer for everything one day. The premises were demolished in 1969.

Workers at the Harbutt Plasticine works, Bathampton.

AT WORK

The 'topping out' ceremony at Bath Corporation's multi-deck car park in Walcot Street. Bill Gibbs (left), site agent, poured beer watched by Brian Beazer. June 1972.

Candlelit shopping.

Young apprentices at the Stothert & Pitt factory gate in January 1989. More than 350 workers lost their jobs when the 150-year-old engineering company closed its factory five months later.

AT WORK

Stothert & Pitt typing pool.

Skilled machinists at work in the factory of Charles Bayer & Co. Ltd.

Staff at Colmers, the department store in Union Street.

AT WORK

In October 1970, Bath clippies were offered tuition to drive the buses. The women turned down the offer, saying they preferred remain on the platform. The photograph shows Mrs Freda Icott, Mrs Phil Rixon and Mrs Frances Farmer.

In April 1962, Alex Moulton (extreme right), who revolutionised world cycling from his Bradford on Avon factory, was awarded the Queen's Award for Industry. He was photographed with his production team who produced the small wheeled bike which was ideal for travelling around the increasingly busy roads.

The Bath Garage, in James Street West, was opened in November 1967 by Raymond Baxter of the BBC. It was the first garage in the West Country to offer a diagnostic service while you waited.

Mrs Edith Sparrow, widow of George Sparrow, founder of Sparrows Crane company, moved the first shovel full of soil on a site alongside Sparrows Crane Hire premises at Lower Bristol Road, Bath in September 1974. Mrs Sparrow is helped by her grandchildren Paul Phelps and Jarrod Waring.

AT WORK

American gaming machine expert Edward J. Drynski (left), flew in from Chicago to give a seminar. The event, in September 1963, was organised by Peter Simper (right) whose firm distributed gaming machines in South West England.

The latest thing from Japan, an electric 'Baby-Kart'. Imported by Peter Simper and Company, of Milk Street, Bath. Demonstrated here by Susan Fysh, of Oldfield Park. Operated by a coin in the slot, the 12-volt baby-kart attracted a lot of interest from stores and holiday camps.

A new-style motor-cycle patrol was introduced to the city when the Bath Police took delivery of three new 650cc BSA bikes, complete with white paint, radio, flashing blue lights and a red stop sign.

AT WORK

The opening of Bath Co-operative Society's new bakery extension at Melcombe Road, by Viscount Alexander of Hillsborough (fourth from right). Left to right are Mrs Brotherton, Mr A.E. Lovick, Mrs Regan, Mr Harding, Mrs Dangerfield, Mr A.H. McCloud, Mr V. Evans, Mr H.W. Nation and Mr W.H. Cox (general manager).

September 1966. Some of the big party of Ministry of Defence (navy department) staff who left Bath Spa Station in two special sleepers to travel to Barrow in Furness for the launching of the first British Polaris submarine, HMS Resolution. The launch was performed by the Queen Mother.

Early 1960s. St John Ambulance volunteers make a collection from spectators on Bath's Recreation Ground.

Admiralty staff, evacuated from Whitehall in the Second World War, arriving in the city and being shown to their temporary accommodation. They arrived by special train and many were billeted with familes across the city who were paid one guinea to cover a week's accommodation, bed and breakfast and evening meals.

Chapter Five
⇜ AT PLAY ⇝

Bathonians have always known how to enjoy themselves and throughout the decades clubs and societies, teams, individuals and families have all been captured by *The Chronicle* photographers simply enjoying life.

Male cast members of Bath Operatic Dramatic Society (B.O.D.S) of Oklahoma *in March 1963.*

Female cast members line up for Oklahoma.

'Ali' and 'Annie' strike a pose during rehearsals for Oklahoma.

AT PLAY

Nowhere to play. By 1957 Snow Hill's 11-storey 'skyscraper' was completed, but there were no play areas for the children. This gang found their fun on the waste land.

BATH – *The Golden Years*

Sunbathers and swimmers in the River Avon near Pulteney Bridge.

Swimmers in Pulteney Weir.

AT PLAY

Above and right: *Swimmers in the Roman Baths.*

The Roman Baths were open for public bathing only during the Bath Festival, a tradition which started in 1961. The Festival Ball that year was a Roman orgy – a Roman feast of Ludi Sulis – held at the baths. It was the first time in living memory people could swim in the baths. Guests at the ball were issued with togas and a Roman feast was offered to diners including boar, roast swan and fired dormice. When the last revellers refused to leave the water at 4 am, the city authorities pulled the plug out of the baths.

Fireworks at the Recreation Ground, August 1981.

Armed with his umbrella the city parks director, Fred Daw, showed two judges, Mr Hare and Mr Conn, the Parade Gardens display for the Britain in Bloom contest. On that day, in September 1969, it rained almost non-stop. The three-man judging team even had difficulty landing their eight-seater plane at Colerne. Bath was hoping to win the national trophy for the third time.

AT PLAY

A city centre display for the Britain in Bloom competition, 1970.

Members of the Bath Rugby team join in the fun for Children in Need, November 1990.

Coffee al fresco in front of the Abbey, June 1966.

AT PLAY

The Silver Ring Choir led by conductor Kelvin Thomas.

Nurses celebrate the Queen's Silver Jubilee in June 1977.

Pupils from Twerton Primary School visit the House of Commons in June 1968.

AT PLAY

Right and below: *Children making the most of the weekend sunshine at Cleveland Baths.*

Mrs M.E. Harmsworth of Bathampton and her dog, which won three first prizes at the West of England and South Wales Airedale Terrier Club show. She also won a second and a third prize at the show staged in St Peter's Church Hall in Lower Bristol Road.

Left: Tall man Nicky B, brushes up on a little light entertainment at the Bath Festival picnic in June 1985.

Below: The theme that year was Pygmalion and this group, dressed in Edwardian-style outfits, called themselves the My Fair American Ladies.

AT PLAY

Dancers in the HTV West go-go dance contest at the Octagon, September 1970. The company was looking for couples to take part in a new weekly programme.

Frankie Vaughan appeared at the Pavilion in October 1958. He arrived half an hour late, accompanied by a police escort, and was forced to battle his way through the crowded hall to his dressing room. He performed his latest single, 'Am I Wasting my Time on Yooooo?'

AT PLAY

Bath Fiesta June 1972 organised by the Bath Round Table. 'Coronation Street' star Pat Phoenix judging the entries in the fancy dress parade at the Recreation Ground.

The carnival procession passing through crowd-lined street at Grand Parade.

Entrants in the carnival pram race accelerate from the starting grid in Royal Victoria Park. It was won by a team from Kingswood.

Chapter Six
CHANGING LANDSCAPES

The blitz on Bath destroyed 329 homes and shops, led to the demolition of another 700 structures and damaged a further 19,000.

Over the years, many buildings of historical significance were restored, the Francis Hotel, and the ancient Abbey Church House, sweeping Somerset Place and the Assembly Rooms. But elsewhere the bomb damage was an opportunity for the planners to tear down areas of the Georgian city and replace them with modern office and tower blocks in what was dubbed the Sack of Bath.

During the decades following the war, much of the unique landscape of historic Bath disappeared and the skyline of the city slowly changed.

Box Station January 1965. Station master W.J. Talbot tends the gas-lamps before the closure of the station.

Prefabs at Wedmore Park. The centrally-heated aluminium kit homes were constructed after the war. Only meant to last ten years, they had been home to many but they were deteriorating rapidly by the early 1960s.

The kitchens were fitted out with fridge, sink, electric boiler, electric cooker, cupboards.

CHANGING LANDSCAPES

Above and right: *Southgate area of Bath.*

Hiskens Bakery, May 1963.

CHANGING LANDSCAPES

Carrying out repairs to the Angel Hotel.

The new Woolworths shop.

CHANGING LANDSCAPES

Green Park Station, Charles Street Post Office.

Afternoon activity at Green Park Station, April 1954. The 40697 on the left leaves with the 4.26pm to Bournemouth and the 40509 waits to form the 4.37pm to Templecombe, while on the right the 41240 removes carriages from an earlier arrival.

Rebecca Fountain undergoing some delicate titivation.

Eileen's Seed Shop in Northumberland Place.

Milsom Street with two-way traffic.

CHANGING LANDSCAPES

Kingsmead Square, March 1963.

In November 1962 the old Scala cinema in Oldfield Park opened its doors as a supermarket.

'Self-service' shoppers queued to pay at the check-out at the Scala supermarket.

CHANGING LANDSCAPES

Jack Allen's Cafe. The cafe ceased trading in Holloway in March 1963, after eighty years.

Bottom of Holloway showing the shops which would all soon cease trading after being bought-up by Bath Corporation in readiness for their demolition.

Demolished buildings in Holloway, 1970s.

Workmen clearing rubble from a demolished building in Holloway.

CHANGING LANDSCAPES

Looking down Holloway. The Young Fox pub (left) which stood on a site tucked away from the main road since long before 1650. The Fox was a popular centre for hundreds of darts and skittle fans.

The Young Fox pub.

Removing the post box from Milsom Street, 1971.

CHANGING LANDSCAPES

The Workmans Rest, Holloway.

Stothert & Pitt Works, August 1981, Pitman Press on Lower Bristol Road.

Royal Sailor pub, Holloway, looking up to Wells Road. Demolished for the Churchill Bridge improvement.

Taken from a passing train in 1960, Royal Sailor, Wells Road, Holloway.

CHANGING LANDSCAPES

Wallace The Cycleries, 1960s. This corner on Lansdown Road and The Paragon has seen many different businesses over the years. Just visible is the Lansdown Arms in Fountain Buildings; this pub still remains.

The George & Dragon pub at Batheaston accepting delivery of a giant barrel.

CHANGING LANDSCAPES

It's the new novelty barrel door installed by workmen, Frank Gay and Alfred Bolton (back row), and Hinge and Jim Finlay, who enjoyed a pint of 'home brew' after their hard work.

Charles Street showing the junction of James Street West, mid 1960s. The houses in Charles Street were all demolished. This junction now houses Bath Social Services department.

Department store in Union Street, September 1962. Colmers first opened a store in 1870. The motto of the shop was 'Sterling value, small profits, no credit.'

CHANGING LANDSCAPES

In March 1954 it was announced that the dry arch on the Bath to Warminster road in Bathampton was to be demolished. Some of the stone was taken to London and used on building work at Buckingham Palace.

Bathwick Hill, April 1971, showing on the left the long-gone A. Richardson & Sons.

December 1968, the Forbes Fraser Hospital on the park site of the RUH. Named after the eminent Bath surgeon who died of blood poisoning after he was pricked by a septic bone while performing an operation.

CHANGING LANDSCAPES

The entrance to the old electricity building in Dorchester Street, Bath.

September 1966. An unusual view of the demolition of the old electricity works.

Southgate area, 1973.

CHANGING LANDSCAPES

H. & R. Hughes.

Pickfords travel agents. Abbeygate Street before the Marples Ridgeway development in the mid 1980s. The area had a whole new look which saw Eric Snook's toy emporium move in. A travel merger in 1993 with Hogg Robinson, Pickfords and Hourmont Travel gave us the travel chain Going Places.

The Royal Oak, known as Rossiter's free house after the landlord, Alderman Bill Rossiter, took over the lease.

Chapter Seven
⚘ FAMILIAR FACES ⚘

Bath has played host to a myriad of famous faces. The city has attracted numerous celebrity visitors and there have been many Bath-born celebrities who have achieved widespread recognition.

Alongside these people we pay tribute to the local characters, the flower seller and *The Chronicle* vendor who are fondly remembered by those who came across them regularly during the course of their day-to-day life.

Two pals meet up again. Percy Thrower was BBC's TV gardener and Fred Daw was Bath's parks director. They were both giving advice to gardeners at Whiteway Garden Centre in June 1974. Percy Thrower trained at The Royal Gardens, Windsor at the same time Fred Daw trained at The Royal Gardens, Sandringham and the two had kept in touch since.

One of Bath's best-known paper sellers, Bill Cottle, retired just before his seventieth birthday. His first patch was outside the old Mineral Water Hospital and he later moved to Terrace Walk close to the Empire Hotel. During the war he was a night watchman at The Chronicle *offices.*

Competitors in a fancy dress competition had a special visitor in July 1973, actress Liz Frazer, who was appearing at The Bath Theatre Royal.

Michael Aspel interviewing young 'Crackerjack' fans.

BATH – *The Golden Years*

September 1962. Alderman Bill Rossiter, licensee of The Royal Oak in Widcombe for nearly fifty years. He was known to many people as a Father Christmas publican. Over the years The Royal Oak had been the centre of activities varying from skittles, dog and pigeon shows, to a cinema club.

FAMILIAR FACES

Paul and Linda McCartney arrive for a private viewing of Linda's Sixties exhibition staged at the Royal Photographic Society in Milsom Street in October 1992.

Ian Botham with members of the Temple Cloud team, winners of the North Somerset Youth Cricket League championship. He presented the team with the Somerset Wyverns trophy at Bath Recreation Ground in June 1985.

On 20 July, 1950 Sir Winston Churchill was made an honorary freeman of Bath. He is pictured with the Mayor, Cllr Miss Kathleen Harper, who was Bath's first woman mayor.

Mrs Davies, who many will remember, sold flowers for a great number of years in the city centre.

Reita Faria, Miss World 1966, visited Bath in March 1967. The attractive Indian medical student spoke to seven-year-old patient Wendy Hooper, at Bath and Wessex Orthopaedic Hospital.

Winston the dog pictured in October 1976.

FAMILIAR FACES

October 1970. Charlie the Jack Russell dog, named after the Prince of Wales, enjoyed a lift on his master's moped. Charlie belonged to painter and decorator John Roberts of Park Street.

Bath City player manager, William Tout, whose football career spanned twenty-three years and included spells with Bristol Rovers and Swindon. When he hung up his football boots he took to the whistle – but not as a referee – as licensee at The Hat and Feather in Walcot Street. He seldom shouted time; instead he used his whistle for the final drink with no extra time.

Librarians from across the South West lined up in The Pump Room to vie for the title of Miss Book World 1969. The winner, seated centre, was nineteen-year-old Maria Johnson, a Bristol librarian from Shirehampton. Local entrants included Oldfield schoolgirl Janet Way, Mrs Wendy White of Berkeley Place, Bath, and Miss Margaret Stott from Odd Down. Contestants were judged on charm, personality and their love of books.

The pop star, Cat Stevens, tried a hat on salesgirl Tessa Bell during the opening party at the Funny Girl boutique. Director of the Bath boutique, Angela Moseley (left) and fellow salesgirls Ana Langrish (right) and Ethlin Drummond watched closely.

FAMILIAR FACES

'Coronation Street's' Len Fairclough, Peter Adamson in real life, opened the new Co-operative Store at Oldfield Park in November 1962.

Leslie Crowther was in town for Bath's carnival in July 1981. He posed with the ladies of Kingsmead Square. More than 50,000 people lined the streets to watch the procession of floats.

Marina Jane and Judith Barclay give jazz man Acker Bilk the VIP treatment at the Bath Conservatives' dinner dance held at the Guildhall in November 1970.

Tony Book, one of Bath City's legendary players, made a welcome return to his home village of Peasedown St John.

FAMILIAR FACES

Peter Ustinov signed copies of his autobiography at Bath Theatre Royal in January 1989. A fund-raising party for showbiz stars and members of the public was followed by a one-man show by Ustinov.

Lord Snowdon visited the construction site of the Walcot Car Park in 1972.

Viv Richards signed autographs for young cricket enthusiasts in 1982.

Freddie and the Dreamers at Longleat in August 1965.

Mr and Mrs Stan Hiskens, familiar to shoppers at Hiskens bakery.

FAMILIAR FACES

1971 and Mick Jagger, who was staying in The Priory Hotel in Weston after a concert in Bristol, visited the Roman Baths and Pump Room with girlfriend Bianca. He went unrecognised by shoppers despite arriving in a cream Bentley and wearing a loud black and white check suit. Two months later the couple married.

BATH – *The Golden Years*

Molly Gerrard, the Bath architect who was involved in many developments in Bath. In 1971 she became the first woman president of Bath Rugby Football Club. This picture from the early 1960s tells the ladies of Bath how to protect their floors, by wearing corks from whisky bottles on their stilettos.

In April 1970 Bath presented all the city's former Mayoresses with brooch as a token of appreciation. The Mayor of Bath, Cllr Alexander S. Polson, who made the presentation in the Banqueting Room at the Guildhall, following a tea, said it was a unique occasion.

FAMILIAR FACES

The Beatles outside the Francis Hotel, June 1963.

Jimi Hendrix at Bath Pavilion in the late 1960s.

Chapter Eight
THE WEATHER

Like most of the country Bath often suffered from severe winters. During January 1963 the River Avon froze over completely, the ice was an inch thick in front of Pulteney Weir, the temperature overnight dropped to minus 8°C and a blanket of snow lay on the ground for weeks. Sledges were used to ferry essential supplies to hospitals and the Co-operative Society suffered a milk bottle shortage as empties vanished in the snow. Again in the early 1980s the weather was back with vengeance. In 1981 blizzards and drifting snow caused havoc on the roads and many homes were without electricity and water for four days and, again, in 1982, 7 inches of snow brought the city to a standstill.

The city also suffered from extensive flooding for many years before the introduction of the flood prevention scheme in the 1970s. In December 1960, heavy rain raised the level of the Avon to 17 feet above normal at the old bridge at the bottom of Southgate Street and the overflowing waters rushed up as far as James Street West.

The problem was solved after the old Pulteney Weir was replaced by the current horseshoe weir and a system of lock gates which could be opened to relieve pressure up river. The Old Bridge, which was partly blamed for the flooding problems, was demolished in 1964 and replaced temporarily by the Wessex Bridge, until the new Churchill Bridge was completed.

Mr Arthur Harrop mops up his shop in Weston Village, October 1960.

Mr G. Mealing in the canoe he used to rescue birds from a flooded fowl house in his garden at Bathampton Bridge toll-house. October 1960.

THE WEATHER

October 1960. 'Bathford Ferry' – a good Samaritan giving a party of Bathford people a lift across the flooded road under the railway arch.

July 1960. Onlookers on The Old Bridge, with Broad Quay in the background, watch the water rise.

View of The Abbey, with snow piled up in front of the Pump Room. Winter 1962.

The only way to get around, carry your shopping on a sledge. Abbey Church Yard.

THE WEATHER

One of the vehicles used by Bath Corporation pushing a track clear in the Upper Borough Walls.

Problems for drivers attempting to find the kerb when parking at South Parade Bath.

Paper seller at the Odeon, Southgate, during the floods in July 1968.

THE WEATHER

Clearing up after the floods at Montrose Cottages, Weston. July 1968.

BATH – *The Golden Years*

Flood damage in Weston. July 1968.

July 1968. Mr John Linfield declared it was business as usual, as the water rose in the London Wine Vaults, Southgate Street.

THE WEATHER

July 1968. The Bath Cricket Festival is a wash out as the Recreation Ground sits under water.

Keynsham floods in 1968.

Flood prevention barriers being erected at Pulteney Weir.

Mrs Phyllis Quintin of School House, Withyditch using her old water pump to help beat the drought in August 1976.

One lane of the Wells Road had to be closed after a crack appearing during the summer drought of 1976.

THE WEATHER

A winter wonderland outside the Abbey in December 1981.

Traffic ground to a halt in wintry Bath in December 1981.

BATH – *The Golden Years*

Len Page holds part of a 10ft icicle which he discovered on the corner of his building in Bathwick during the great British freeze in 1982.

Children tobogganing in Upper Church Street. 1982.

THE WEATHER

Children of Burford Close, Southdown played in an igloo built by their friends, Ian Dagger and Ian Wheeler, using blocks of frozen snow which were dug up when the cul-de-sac was cleared.

BATH – *The Golden Years*

Commuters arriving at Bath Spa station faced a slow trek along snowy pavements to reach their offices. 1982.

Roy Robinson solved the problem of how to get to work. He skied to his job at Pitman Press. 1982.

Chapter Nine
ᘛ SPORT ᘚ

Like any big city Bath has numerous sports teams, both professional and amateur. Local works teams such as Stothert & Pitt and the boys' teams from The Percy Boys Club will be remembered fondly by many Bathonians.

Bath City Football Club, founded in 1889, played their early games on the Recreation Ground in the city centre and Bath Rugby fixtures still attract a large attendance at the ground. Somerset County Cricket Club use the ground during the annual summer Cricket Festival.

Several local youngsters have achieved national and international recognition – Tony Book, John Hall, and Jason Gardener among others.

Bath City's chairman Alex Brown looks on as Eddie Hapgood ties on a lucky mascot at the start of the 1951–52 season for good luck.

Bath City team 1951–52 season, just before setting off for an away game.

BATH – *The Golden Years*

It's an away day for the fans, 8 January 1964. A convoy of 14 coaches carrying nearly 600 Bath City supporters left Bath bus station for Bolton, for the FA cup replay.

18 October 1952 on Bath Recreation Ground. No games attracted more interest than the Bath v Bristol encounters. This time – Bath were victorious, thanks to former Bristol player, Paddy Sullivan's three penalty goals.

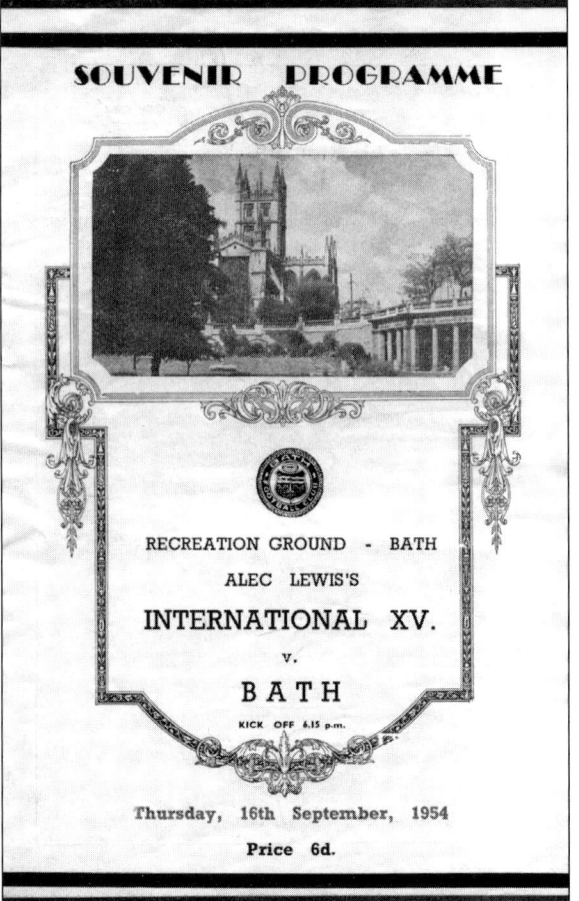

Souvenir programme Thursday 16 September 1954. Alec Lewis's International XV v Bath. Picture shows Bath Abbey from Parade Gardens.

SPORT

John Player Special Cup final, Twickenham April 26, 1986. Bath v Wasps. Bath won their third successive JPS cup final. Bath 25 Wasps 17.

Left and below: *Bath v Llanelli on the Recreation Ground, September 1946. It was a draw 3–3.*

Players in left image, left to right: *D.S. Beard, Joe Bailey, M.J. Howell, H.V. Bland (with ball), Tommy Hicks and Stan Ascott (far right).*

Players in image below, left to right: *D.S. Beard, G.R. Speke, Len Harter, H.V. Bland, M.J. Howell and Joe Bailey.*

BATH – *The Golden Years*

Fancy dress on the Rec. A regular fund-raiser, which dates back to 1879. This more recent photograph shows Walcot Old Boys RFC who set the theme to commemorate Queen Elizabeth's Coronation in 1953.

What me Ref? Former paratrooper Roger Spurrell took over the Bath Rugby Club captaincy in 1982. The picture shows Spurrell (number 6), supported by England International Paul Simpson.

Right, both images: *Wrestling. The Pavilion was used for many things, but one of the weekly highlights was the wrestling bout. Here two wrestlers get to grips, and the second picture shows the crowd getting into the spirit of cheering them on. March 1971.*

SPORT

In May 1989 Beechen Cliff School Bath were optimistic that this thirteen-year-old athlete would go all the way. Jason Gardener, England's Olympic sprinter, is known locally as the Bath Bullet.

Young Fox skittle team. Mid 1960s. The Young Fox was one of the last pubs to go in Holloway.

Gillian Gifford tests the water at Beau Street Baths. The long-established Bath Dolphins Women's swimming club was competing in the autumn gala.

SPORT

October 1963. Meet the golfing Green family. L-R Paul, Peter, Mrs Green, Mr Ken Green, and in front showing how it's done three-year-old old Kelvin, who already had his own clubs. Peter Green was Bath Golf Club's first international golfer.

Bath Triathlon. September 1993. Swimmers on the first leg of the race swim on the River Avon below Pulteney Weir. Spectators watch from Parade Gardens.

SPORT

Landsdown Men's and Ladies' cricket teams. June 1971.

Panoramic view of cricket on the Recreation Ground.

J.C. White leading Somerset out to field against Yorkshire at Bath. J.C. White was a great personality in the game. A county player from 1909–1937, during which period he claimed 2000 wickets and scored 11,375 runs.

BATH – *The Golden Years*

June 1988. Somerset Ladies Bowling Association celebrated their sixtieth anniversary with a special match at the Bloomfield Bowling Club in Bath. The diamond jubilee contest between Somerset ladies and the county's executive officers was part of a series of events to mark the formation of the club, the oldest ladies' bowling association in England.

SPORT

June 1967. Lady Strathcona starting J. Boncombe and P.A.W. Stephens from the Bath Garages as they set off to compete in the Bath Motor Club Festival.

November 1976. Excitement as the first car roars away from the grid down Great Pulteney Street, Bath, at the start of the 2000-mile Lombard RAC Rally.

Jubilant Percy Boys U14's Reserves win the Sunday Youth Football League final at Twerton Park, April 1978.